Safed the Sage

Safed
the
Sage

BY WILLIAM E. BARTON

JOHN KNOX PRESS
ATLANTA

10   9   8   7   6   5   4   3

INTERNATIONAL STANDARD BOOK NUMBER: 0-8042-3424-8
LIBRARY OF CONGRESS CATALOG CARD NUMBER: 65-13377
COPYRIGHT © 1965 BY M. E. BRATCHER
PRINTED IN THE UNITED STATES OF AMERICA

CONTENTS

Safed the Sage

The Dog and the Limited

Now I rode on a Fast Express Train called the Limited. And we went through a Country where there were Many Farms. And the Train went like the Driving of Jehu.

And there was a Farmhouse that stood near unto the track but back, as it were, about the space of a Furlong. And in the Farmhouse dwelt a Farmer. And the Farmer had a Dog. And when the Train drew Nigh, the Dog started from the Farmhouse toward the Train. And he Barked Furiously, and he Ran Swiftly. And I marveled that he could run so Swiftly, and that at the same time he could Bark so Furiously. But with all his barking he could not make so much Noise as the Train, neither with all his Running could he overtake it.

And the path that he made in his Running was a Great Parabolic Curve. For he started before the Train entered the Farm, running toward the Train, and going East, for the Train was toward the West. But as the Train ran on and stopped not, the Dog ran South, and when the Train was going By and not even Hesitating, he Curved so that he ran Southwest and then West. And at the west side of the Farm he fell into a Ditch, and rolled over and over and got up, and shook himself, and stood for a moment and cursed the Train, and then Returned Home.

And the Train went on.

And a month thereafter I rode on the same Train, and behold, the Same Dog did all the Things that he had done before.

And three months thereafter I rode again on the Same Train, and the Same Fool Dog was still Getting Experience in the Same Manner, but Learning Nothing Therefrom.

And I saw that he was even like unto some Men, who might be Brayed in a Mortar with a Pestle, yet would not their Folly depart from them.

For even as that Dog watcheth daily for that Train, rising every morning and listening for it, and chasing it through the Farm, and Tumbling in the Ditch on the West Line of the Farm, so there are Men who Chase their Follies Continually, and learn Nothing from their Tumbles.

And what would the Dog have Done with the Train if he had Caught it?

The Man from Jonesville

Now, there was among my Neighbors a man whose name was Smith, and he was from Jonesville. And he told me often of Jonesville, what a Lovely Place it was, and how every one who lived there was Happy and Virtuous, and how sorry he was that he ever had left there, and how he wanted to go back to Jonesville. And when the men in the city where I lived failed to clean the Snow off their Sidewalks, or the City Council indulged in Graft, or the children were Rude, or there was an Early Frost, he told me that Such Things did not happen in Jonesville. And this continued for nigh unto Twenty Years;

and the older he grew the more he talked about Jonesville. And I told him I hoped that when he died he would go to Jonesville.

Now it came to pass that he prospered, so that he retired from Business. And he sold his House and Lot in the City wherein I dwell, and went back to Jonesville that he might Spend his Last Years in Peace, and Die in Jonesville. And we all Bade him Farewell, with something of Sorrow, and Something of Relief.

And it came to pass that at the end of Six Months, he and his Wife moved back again, and bought back their Old House for a Thousand Dollars more than they sold it for. And they were Tenfold more Happy to get back than they had been to go away.

And it came to pass on an Evening that Keturah and I called on them. And I said, Old Fellow, tell me on the Level, what was the matter with Jonesville?

And he said to me, Speak not to me of Jonesville, lest I do thee Harm. It is the toughest Joint this side of States Prison. The dear people we knew have all died or moved away, and they who are in their places are Unneighborly and Snobbish. And they do Outrageous Dances and other Stunts, and their Kids are the Limit. We have come back to Dwell in the place where we have spent Twenty Happy Years, and we have but one favor to ask of our old Neighbors, and that is, that they never speak to us of Jonesville.

And as Keturah and I walked home, I spake to her, and said, Keturah.

And Keturah answered, I know what thou art about to say; and I suspected all the time that it would be just so.

And I said, There are many men and women who sigh for some Jonesville or other, who might be Decently

Happy where they are if they would make it their business.

And Keturah said, Our Jonesville is right here.

And I said, Amen.

The Curves and the Tangents

I rode in the Cab of a Locomotive, and I spake with
the man who drave the Engine, and we went at High
Speed. And High Speed is one thing from the rear end of
the Observation Car, and Quite Another Thing from the
Cab of a Locomotive; and it giveth a man the Impression
that he is not running a Sewing Machine.

And I looked out upon the Track.

And I spake unto the Engineer, and I said, Behold,
how many are the Curves; whereas, the Map which this
Company doth print with its Time Table doth shew the
Road to be a Straight Line Joining every Great City in
America to every other Great City.

And he said, That is how it looketh on the map; but to
the engineer every railroad is a Double System of Curves,
the Curves on the Surface and the Curves Up and Down.
A railroad curves to get a better approach to a bridge, or
to enter a town, or to avoid a swamp or an hill, or to go
around the land of some Farmer who tried to sell his
land at four prices, so there is a Curve to the right and a
Tangent, and then a Curve to the left; and sometimes
there is a Reverse Curve with no Tangent between, in
which case the Passenger doth think Unkind Thoughts of
the Engineer without knowing why he is jerked Galley-

West. Believe me, the business of running an air ship like this is something more than opening and shutting the Throttle, for there are always the Curves to pull around and see around, and thou dost never know what doth lie in wait around the rim of the Curve, nor how strongly the Train will be tempted to disregard the Curve and survey a new Tangent of its own.

And I said, What is the other system of Curves?

And he said, No roadbed is level. Even in a Prairie Country, the roadbed descendeth to a little stream, and ascendeth to a little hill, and then descendeth to a larger stream, and ascendeth to a larger hill; and it must all be considered in terms of Coal Consumption, and Steam Pressure, and the Weight of the Train, and the Condition of the Track whether it be Dry or Wet or Frosty.

And I said, Thou hast many things to trouble thee that I wot not of.

And he said, Passengers mostly think that all an Engineer hath to do is to keep the train between the Fences of the Right of Way, and get in on Time. Behold, they consider not the Curves of either class. For a Railway is not all Tangents.

And I considered and said, Thy business is like unto mine. For there be Railroad men who think that I have only to stand in the Pulpit one day in seven, and open my mouth and the Lord will fill it. Behold, there are curves as well as Tangents on my Right of Way, yea, Reverse Curves, and some Heavy Grades.

And he said, I reckon it is so with every man's business. Though to another man it looketh like a Straight Line surveyed across the Map, yet to him that is on the inside, every business hath not only its Tangents but its Curves.

And we took each other by the Right Hand, and we bowed low and said our Salaams, and I bade him Farewell and Departed. And each of us knew that the other man's job was like unto his own.

The Doughnut

Now I entered the Kitchen, and would have passed through. But Keturah was there; so I waited: and she cast Divers Things into a Great Bowl, and did stir them with a Great Spoon.

And I asked her, saying, What hast thou in the Bowl?

And she said, Sugar and Spice, and all that's nice.

And I said, That is what God used when He made thee.

And she took the Dough out of the Bowl, when she had stirred it, and she rolled it with a Rolling-Pin; and she cut it into round cakes. And in the midst of every several cake was there an Hole. And a great Caldron hung above the Fire, and there was Fat therein and it boiled furiously.

And Keturah took the round Cakes of Dough, and cast them into the Caldron; and she poked them with a Fork, and she turned them, and when they came forth, behold I knew then what they were. And the smell of them was inviting, and the appearance of them was exceeding good. And Keturah gave me one of the Doughnuts, and Believe Me, they were Some Doughnuts.

And I said, To what purpose is the Hole? If the Doughnut be so good with a part Punched Out, how much better had it been if the Hole also had been Doughnut?

And Keturah answered and said, Thou speakest as a Foolish Man, who is never content with the goodness that is, but always complaineth against God for the lack of the Goodness which he thinketh is not. If there were no Hole in the Doughnut, then were it like unto Ephraim, a cake not turned. For, though the Cake were Fried till the Edges thereof were burnt and hard as thy Philosopher's Stone, yet would there be uncooked Dough in the middle. Yea, thou shouldest then break thy teeth on the outer rim of every Several Doughnut, and the middle part thereof would be Raw Dough.

And I meditated much on what Keturah had told me. And I considered the Empty Spaces in Human life; and the Desolation of its Vacancies; and how men's hearts break over its Blank Interstices. And I pondered in my soul whether God doth not know that save for these, our lives would be like unto Ephraim.

And I spake of these things to Keturah, and she said, My lord, I know not the secret of these mysteries. Yea, mine own heart acheth over some of the Empty Places. But say unto the sons of men that he who useth not the good things which he hath but complaineth against his God for those he lacketh, is like unto a man who rejecteth a Doughnut because he Knoweth not the Mystery of the Hole.

The Man in the Upper Berth

There was a day when I took a journey, and I rode in a Car of Juggernaut, even a Sleeping Car. And I had bought my railway Ticket and my Pullman Ticket, and paid the Tax thereon. And I had a Lower Berth, and was content.

And there came into the Car a Passenger who had a Ticket for an Upper Berth. And he was wroth. And he Spake much concerning it, so that all that were in the Car heard what he said. And he spake saying:

I'd like to know what kind of a One Horse Road this is that can't put on Cars enough to give its Patrons Decent Service. For I have never slept before in an Upper Berth, and I like it not.

Now, the man who hath never slept in an Upper Berth hath not slept many times in a Lower Berth. And I looked at the Passenger, and I suspected that it was from Motives of Economy he had taken the Upper Berth, and that if he had bought a Lower Berth he would have gone Without Breakfast.

Wherefore I let him talk till he had told all who were in the car how sad he was at having to sleep in an Upper Berth. And I said to him:

I have a ticket for a Lower Berth, and it cost me One Dollar more than an Upper Berth, and the Tax is another Dime. I will Exchange Berths with thee, and thou mayest give to me a Dollar and Ten Cents.

And he began with shame to Side Step mine offer. And he said, I could not think of accepting a Favor at the expense of thy Comfort.

And I said, I shall be Comfortable in the Upper Berth,

and the more so for the Comfort thou art to have in the Lower One.

And I called to the Ethiopian who accompanied that Chariot, and I said, Move my things to Upper Seven, and give this man Lower Six; and come thou with thy Fire Escape, and I will go up.

But the Passenger began to Sweat, so that Cold Drops stood on his Forehead, and he said,

I thank thee just as much, but I am Running a Little Short on my Expense Account; and if it is all the same to thee, I will Go Up Stairs and save my Dollar Ten.

And I said, Peace go with thee.

And the other Passengers began to Snigger.

And he Went Up Very Soon, and was glad to go.

And one of the Other Passengers came nigh unto me, and he Laughed, and said,

Thou didst Sure Get His Number.

And I said, The man who hath Little at home is the man who Kicketh when he goeth abroad. And he who Complaineth Loudly at the Small Discomforts of Travel is he who is Getting all he is paying for, and more than he can afford.

And he said, I had not thought of it on this wise, but I verily believe thou art right.

Having Enough

There spake to me a man who said, My income is not enough.

And I said, Thou art a Fortunate Man.

And he said, Why dost thou say so?

And I said, Because thou hast the choice either of Earning More or Spending Less; and when there be two ways of solving a problem, a man is Fortunate. Whereas I know a Poor Man who Owneth a Railroad and Earnestly Coveteth Another; he is Poor, for he cannot get it.

And he said, When I was a lad, I drove my father's cow to an Hired Pasture, for we lived in a Little Town. And other men in the same town besought me to drive their cows, and they gave me every one of them Ten Cents a Week; and their Cows were Five. And I thought How Happy I should be if there were Ten Cows and I could earn Every Week an Whole Dollar. And when I became older, of about the age of Fourteen, then did I hire myself in the springtime to a Farmer to Plant Potatoes; and we cut the Seed Potatoes so that on Every Piece there were Two Eyes, and we planted Forty Acres of them. And we dropped the potatoes where the Marker had crossed the soft furrow, one potato for every step as we walked, and with the eyes up, and we stepped on each potato as we walked to press it firmly into the soft earth. And I worked for him Eleven Days, and received Five Dollars and the Half of a Dollar; and I reflected that if Potato Planting could last All Summer then might I earn Thirteen Dollars every Month. And the year I was Seventeen, I hired myself to an Husbandman from the eighteenth day of the sixth month to the first day of the eleventh month for Eighty Dollars, which was almost Sixteen Dollars a month. And when the eleventh month came, I drew my money, and bought me a New Suit of Clothes with a pair of Gorgeous Suspenders and a Beautiful Necktie, yea and a wondrous Overcoat and a pair

of Dogskin Gloves which I called Kid. And I had Forty
Seven Dollars left, and it was too much to trust to Any
One Bank, lest it Break.

And I said to him, What is thine Income Now?

And he said, The Government of the United States
hath lately asked me the Same Question, and when I
told them, they struck me for a sum that made mine Hair
Stand on End. I knew not till then how Poor is the man
who is as Rich as I.

And I said, The Holy Scriptures call down a Blessing
on the man who Considereth the Poor; I will bless also
the man who, however Poor he is, Considereth himself
Rich. For thou wast Rich when thou dravest cows to Pasture, and hast been rich ever since if thy Mind hath been
at peace with God and man and thou hast had enough to
pay thine Honest Debts.

And I spake to him this proverb of the men of Arabia,
Who is richer, he that hath a Million Dollars or he that
hath Seven Daughters?

And he said, Tell me the answer.

And I said, The man who hath Seven Daughters is the
Richer; for he hath enough, and knoweth it.

The Women and Their Carfare

There runneth through the City wherein I reside, a
System of Trolley Cars, and there be those wherein one
shall Pay as he Entereth, and some there be of the Other
Kind. And I was riding in one of the Other Kind. And
over against where I sat were Two Women.

And as they entered, they began both of them Diving

deep, each one of them into her Bag, to find her Purse, or
to Appear to be Trying to Find it. And as they Dove,
each into her own Bag, thus they spake one to another,
saying, Let me pay, I pray thee; Nay, but thou shalt let
me pay; I am sure thou didst pay the last time; it is my
Turn.

And with many such words spake they one to another.

But they found neither of them her Purse.

So they Dove both of them, and talked fast, saying,
Let me pay.

And one of them ceased to Dive, but spake unto the
other, saying, Oh, well, thou mayest pay, and I will pay
the next time.

And the other one was Disappointed, for that was what
she had intended to say, but the first one Beat Her To It.

Then the one who had been permitted to pay quickly
found her purse, and it was Very Small and Very Flat.
And she opened it, and took out One Lone Nickel. And
she began with a Very Red Face to say,

I have enough for Myself; I have not enough for Both
of Us.

Then the first also grew Red in the Face, and she also
found her Purse without any more Deep Diving, and she
also produced a Nickel.

And they paid each of them Her Own Fare.

And there came a Coldness over the Meeting; neither
did they speak much thereafter to each other.

And when I had gone to mine own house, I told this
Event unto Keturah.

And Keturah said, Wherefore shouldest thou delight
in beholding the follies of women? Have men no follies?

And I held my peace.

The Windmill and the Pump

I have a friend who is an Husbandman, and I visited him upon his Farm, and tarried with him one night. And upon his Farm are Cattle and Swine and Horses. And he watereth them from a Deep Well wherein is a Pump, and the Pump runneth by a Windmill.

And it came to pass after Supper that he spake unto a Swede that labored upon the farm, and he said, Ole, there is a Good Breeze tonight; start thou the Windmill.

And the Swede went forth into the Night, and loosened a Rod that runneth up to the Mill, and that holdeth the Tail against the Wheel so that the Wind driveth it not. But when the Rod is loosened, then the Tail swingeth around, and the Wheel cometh into the Wind, and the Wheel turneth to Beat the Band. And ere the Swede had returned to the house, we heard the Wheel running, and my friend said, On the morrow we shall have a Tank full of Water for the Livestock.

Now the room where I slept was on the side of the house toward the Windmill, and when I wakened in the night, it was Running like the Wind, and I said, Verily it will pump the well dry at that rate.

But when we went out in the morning, behold, there was no water. For the Pump had been Disconnected from the Mill, and the Swede saw not in the Darkness that the Connecting Pin was out; wherefore he connected it not. And the mill had run all night and the Tank was empty.

Now when I beheld this, I thought of many men whom I know, whose Windmill goeth around continually, and who are always Creaking their Boots to show that they are Among Those Present, and who talk long and earnestly about Earnestness and Efficiency and the Rest, but it Cutteth no Ice, and it Draweth no Water. Now these be good men, whose minds are Responsive to the Winds of God, and their Capacity for doing something is as Excellent as that of the Pump, but between the Wheels that God driveth and the Pump of their own endeavor, there lacketh an adjustment.

And I have often wondered how it should be that in the mechanism of some good men there would seem to have been evidenced the blunder of some Sleepy Swede, fumbling in the dark, and putting the Wheel in Gear, but failing to connect the Pump. And this is the word that I spake in the ears of men, Count it not a sure sign of efficiency that the Wheel goeth round and the Pump is in order; be thou sure the Wheels of thy Head are hitched to the Pump of thy Performance.

The New Recipe

There was a morning when I rose from my bed, and looked at the sunrise, and thanked God that I was alive, even as I do each day. And I descended and came down, and ate my breakfast. And behold upon the table there were Doughnuts. Now if there be Doughnuts, I eat of them, but they minish not in any wise the other things that I eat, for I eat of them last.

And I said unto Keturah, Hast thou bought Sinkers from the Market? For I had not smelled the cooking of them.

And she said, I have not; for I value my peace of mind and the good will of my husband. I made these. Yea, and I made them by a New Recipe.

And I said, Wherefore wilt thou try New Recipes when already thy Doughnuts are perfect?

And she said, It is not thus that thou dost preach, for thou dost ever exhort men to do better and better.

And I said, Thine aspiration to have things better and better is thine only fault. Thou dost even try to have it so with thy Husband.

And she said, Yea, and thus far I have done very well in the matter of his improvement.

So I ate of the Doughnuts, and I said, Behold, these are just like all of thy Doughnuts.

And she said, I am glad that thou dost think so. For they are so made that they absorb less Fat; therefore are they the more Wholesome.

And I said, Go not too far with me in that Wholesome stunt; I do not want things too Wholesome; I can digest anything save it be Health Foods.

And she said, My lord, when I try a New Recipe, thus do I try it. I consider all the things that I have been wont to use that I know are good, and if I find in the New Recipe some other good thing, that also do I put in.

And I said, Keturah, thou hast the finest idea of Progress to be found in any cook on earth. For thou goest ahead, but thou playest not far from thy Base.

And I said, If all reformers would learn of thee, then would the Millennium come sooner.

And she said, I am glad that thou dost like the new Doughnuts.

And I verily did like them. For they had one ingredient that changeth not, and that is Keturah.

Grindstone and Scythe

There came to me one of the sons of the prophets. And I bade him enter, and he came in and made obeisance and sat down. And he said unto me, I have need of thy wisdom. For I minister to a Little Congregation, and behold they are Stiff-Necked and Hard of Heart. And albeit I preach to them Faithfully, yet do they not heed. Yea, and the more earnestly I preach, the fewer of them come to hear me.

And his heart was hot and sore, and I looked on him and mine heart was sad for him.

And I asked him what he had been preaching about, and what were the duties that he had been exhorting his people to attain unto.

And I discovered that he had an Hobby, which he rode incessantly, so that in nearly every Sermon he did mount it and make at least one circle round the ring. And it did not happen to be the Hobby of his people. Nay, it was of such a nature that they Disliked it and Resented it. And the more he preached on that subject the less they cared to do that duty or any other.

And I said unto him, When I was a lad, I visited my Grandsire, who did live on a farm. And he was an aged man. And he had a Scythe which he desired to sharpen, that he might cut Thistles in the Pasture. And he desired to Grind the Scythe.

And he commanded me to Turn the Grindstone, which I did, but I liked it not.

And my Grandsire was aged, and his sight was not good, and he had left his Glasses in the house.

Now after we had ground the Scythe until it should have been sharp, he took it and looked at the edge thereof, and behold, the edge was like unto that of a Saw.

And he sent me unto the House that I might bring unto him his Glasses, and he examined the Grindstone, and there was in the surface of it a Small Flinty Stone, as large as the head of a Pin. And every time that stone came around, it made a nick in the thin edge of the Scythe. And he took an Hammer and a Cold Chisel, and cut out the Small Flinty Stone. Then did we grind the Scythe again, and the stone ground all parts of the edge evenly so that it was sharp. And it cut the Thistles good and plenty.

And I said unto the son of the prophets, The preacher who hath in his mind any one Notion or Idea or Doctrine or Duty which he feeleth called upon to air in every sermon, behold he is like unto a Grindstone with a Small Flint that maketh a Nick whenever he turneth the Crank.

And I said unto him, Go thou back, and as for the doctrine and duty which thou hast preached so unremittingly, take thy Cold Chisel and from thy sermons of the next year, Cut It Out.

And he had sense enough to follow my Advice; which is not true of all people who come to me that they may obtain it.

And he and his people lived happily ever after.

The Bad Boy

There came to me a Mother, and she said, O Safed, thou great and wise man, have pity on thine hand-maiden, for I am in sorrow. Thou knowest my Boy. He is fourteen years old. When he was a Baby, he was the Cutest Little Thing thou didst ever see.

And I said, I remember.

And she said, And when he was a Little Boy he was lovely.

And I said, Thou speakest truly.

And she said, But now I hardly know him. He is Noisy, and Rude, and Inattentive, and Heedless; and he Learneth not his Lessons, and when I reprove him he laugheth, and saith, I Should Worry. Tell me, O Safed, what shall I do?

And I said, Worry not.

And she said, I cannot help it. Was there ever such a boy?

And I said, George Washington, when he was four-teen, did not always wash himself behind his ears. And Julius Caesar when he was fourteen was not always rev-erent in Sunday School. And William Shakespeare when he was fourteen got excused from his work to attend the funeral of his grandmother, and on that day watched a ball-game. And Simon Peter when he was fourteen was one day absent from school on account of Serious Illness, but recovered sufficiently to watch the bobbing of a cork upon the water of a little creek what runneth into the Sea of Galilee hard by Capernaum.

And she said, Do the books tell of that?

And I said, Nay, but I know that it is so, for I know boys.

And she said, O Safed, it doeth me great good to hear thee; and it restoreth my faith in my boy.

And she rose to go. But she turned back, and she said,

O Safed, when thou wast fourteen, what kind of a boy wast thou?

And I said, If I tell thee that I was a Model thou wilt be sorry to think I was not like other boys; and if I tell thee that I was like other boys thou wilt think I was not a Model. But if I tell thee not, then canst thou have the joy of thinking either of these things or both.

So I bade her Salaam, and she went out.

And it was Lucky for me that she did not ask Keturah.

The River and the Flood

I have a friend who dwelleth in a City that is builded beside a Great River, even the Ohio. And there are times when the Bottom of that River getteth upon the Top so that the Boats have Hard Work not to Puncture their Tires. But there are other times when the River Riseth as Jordan overfloweth all his Banks, and then there is Something Doing.

Now I visited my friend as the Winter drew to an end, and the River began to Rise. And the Ice went out in Great Cakes that swam in the Yellow Water, and the Backwaters were in all the Valleys and over the Lowlands, and the Morning Papers told every day that it was

Two Feet higher at Pittsburgh. And I stood beside the stream, and it flowed in a Wide Yellow Flood that no man could turn aside, and when I went away and came again, behold it washed the bank at a Higher Level. And the water came into the Street of the Town where I was, and still it rose.

And I looked that the men of that city should have showed Fear. But they showed it not. And certain of them whose places of Business were near the Wharfboat spake of the water that was putting out the fires in their Basement, but they Stuck to Business on the Ground Floor, and when the water rose to the Ground Floor, they moved their Papers Upstairs and locked up and Took a Vacation for a few days.

And day by day the water rose, till they did little Business in that town save the moving of property Upstairs and Waiting.

Now I was Anxious, for it seemed as if the River would never Cease Rising. But there came a Morning when the Paper said that the River had fallen Four Inches at Pittsburgh. Now behold it still was rising where we were, and it grew higher all that day and that night, so that the friend whom I visited moved out of his home and took me to the Hotel where he had reserved Rooms for us, and we lodged there. But all men spake cheerfully, for they said, Though it rise another foot tonight, and put out the fires in the Hotel and the Printing Office and the Bank, yet tomorrow will it begin to Go Down.

And it was even as they said.

For I stood next day upon the bank, and the River was miles in Width, but there was a Streak of Mud as it were an handbreadth wide above the water on the Shore. And the people began to Assemble their Mops, and prepare to Clean Up.

Now it was a New Experience to me, but to them it was Familiar. And they knew the power of the water, and they knew the raging of the flood, and they knew that they could not stop it. But they possessed their souls with patience, for they said, It cannot rise forever, and its pride and fury will soon pass.

And I prayed to my God that I might accept life's inevitable trials even as the men of that town accepted the flood.

But if I go to live in that town, I want a Little Rainbow of Mine own.

The Crossing-Tender

Now there is a Railway that runneth through the Town where I live, and there are Gates that are pulled down when a Train Goeth by. And one day when I would have crossed the Tracks, the Gates went down, so that I stopped. And I spake unto the man who keepeth the crossing, and I said, Lovest thou thy Job?

And he said, I count myself lucky to have this Job, for I am neither young nor strong; nevertheless mine is an Hard Job.

And I said, Wherefore should thy Job be Hard?

And he said, Because I save people's lives, and they turn and curse me.

And I said, That is strange, for they should love thee.

And he said, They come down the Street breaking the

Speed Limit, and Honking for me to Lift the gates; or if they be on Foot they Duck Under. And when I warn them not to cross the Tracks lest they die, they act as if I were their Enemy.

And I took him by the Hand, and I said, Thou art my Brother, and my Job is like unto thine.

And he said, Not So You Could See It. Art thou not a Minister and a Philosopher?

And I answered, I am a Crossing-Tender. Where thou seest Yonder Spire, I tend a Crossing; and I say unto the Wicked, Go not in thine Evil Way, lest thou Die, but they continue to go as they did before. And I say unto the Heedless, Duck not under the Gate, lest evil befall thee; but they Duck as they were wont to do.

Now I had on my Best Clothes and the Crossing-Tender had on his Overalls, but we clasped hands, and he knew that we were Brothers. For my lot in life is even as his, and my Job hath the same Trials.

Nevertheless, his is a good Job, and so is Mine. And every now and then we keep people on the Right Side of the Gate.

So I considered this, and I thanked my God for my Job, and I resolved to do it as well as I could.

The Bay Rum

I sat in the shop of a Barber, and the Barber cut my Hair, and trimmed my Beard. And there came a Seller of Barbers' Supplies and spake unto the Barber while the

Barber did things unto me. And the Seller of Barbers'
Supplies spake thus:

Behold, I have brought unto thee a Sample of our New
Brand of Bay Rum, which I wish thee to try, and see if it
be not More Mild than any Bay Rum thou hast ever used.

And the Barber spake unto me, saying, Shall I try it on
thee?

And I said, Go to it. I will Try Anything Once.

And he put the New Brand of Bay Rum upon my Face
and upon my Neck.

And he said to me, How dost thou find it? Is it indeed
Mild?

And I answered, Thou hast said it. It is so mild that I
know not if it be Bay Rum or Rain Water.

And the Seller of Barbers' Supplies answered and said,
If thou must have it Bite, I might have put in Red Pepper.

And I said, Nay, I care not for the Bite in Itself, but it
seemeth to me that the High Cost of Living hath Hit the
Bay Rum Industry, so that the New Brand hath come
from Lake Michigan.

And I said, Mildness is All Right in Its Place. A little
mildness now and then is relished by the Best of Men;
but if I pay Real Money unto the Barber, I desire that
there be some evidence that he giveth me the Real Stuff,
and not something out of the Rain Water Barrel. I would
rather be hurt with something that is to do me Good than
be mollified by that which shall Harm me or Profit me
Nothing.

So I left the shop of the Barber, and I went to mine
House, and I sat me down to prepare Wise Words to
speak to the people on the Sabbath.

And it was in mine heart to speak unto them in all
Gentleness, for I love them, and they are very good to
me. But I heard the voice of God saying unto me, Cry
aloud, spare not, lift up thy voice like a trumpet, and
show my people their transgressions, and this congregation their sins.

And I did as God spake unto me, and I called them to
repentance and a new life.

And they said unto me, Now that was the way to
preach. We desire sermons that have Some Punch in
them.

And I reflected that they would rather be hurt by that
which was to do them good than be pleased with that
which would harm them or profit them nothing.

The Collection of Geniuses

There came to our city a Woman who called often at
the house where we abide, and she counted herself a
friend of Keturah. And I asked of Keturah, saying, Is this
Susie person married or single?

And Keturah answered, Both.

And I said, It is just about what I should have ex-
pected.

And Keturah said, She hath many of the marks of Genius, and she knoweth many persons who are Geniuses.
Yea, and she hath invited us to spend an evening with
her and meet a Group of her Friends, all of whom are
Geniuses in their way.

So we went, I and Keturah, and we spent an evening

in the apartment of Susie. And she trotted out her Geniuses.

And there was a Poetess who wrote Vers Libre so wonderful that it could not be told from Prose. And there was a Musician who played his Violin after a new theory which maintained that Music should have neither Melody nor Harmony nor Key nor Time, but reach the Higher Levels of the Soul through Free Interpretation. And there was an Author, who had writ a Great Book, so profound that no Publisher could understand it or see the need of publishing it. And there was a woman who had a New Theory of Thought-Transmission, and another who would Revolutionize Education by Interpreting Morals in terms of Music, and Music in terms of Color.

And Susie introduced them to us, one by one, and I and Keturah were about the only people there who were not Geniuses. So they began every man and woman of them to tell us their Theories.

And when we came away, we were that weary, we walked not, but ordered a Taxi.

And Keturah said, It was a Great Social Triumph for Susie.

And I answered, Yea.

And Keturah said, And I was Bored.

And I said, So was I, unless there be in the Dictionary some word which meaneth the same and then some.

And I said, Keturah, thou art no Genius; neither am I. But thou art mighty Good and Wondrous Sensible, and I am a Philosopher, which is, being interpreted, a man with Good Ordinary Common Sense.

And Keturah said, An evening with a Choice Assortment of Geniuses is like unto a Feast in a Pickle Factory.

And I said unto her, God hath need of mighty few Geniuses; and as for a job lot like that we have met, it is of the Lord's mercies that they are not consumed. Let us be thankful that in this world are so large a number of Commonplace Sensible Folk.

The Home of the Sparrow

There is a Great City, and there runneth a Street through the midst thereof, and on this side of the Street and on that are High Buildings. And some of them are like unto the Tower of Babel. And one of those buildings is named for the man who Discovered America. And upon the front of the building, even above the Main Entrance, and High above the Sidewalk, is a Graven Image of Christopher Columbus.

And I sat in that Building, beside a Window that looketh out as if Christopher Columbus had stepped through it to where his Image standeth.

And it was Winter. And the wind was Cold, and the snow Blew down the street.

And under the garment of Christopher Columbus, and hard by one of his legs, was a Sparrow. And he had found for himself a place About as Snug and Comfortable as any bird could find out of doors on That Kind of a day. And he was sheltered from the Wind and from the Snow.

And the Sparrow was nigh unto the Window, so that I might almost have put forth my hand and taken him inside, but he was better off where he was. And the Sparrow saw me, and I saw the Sparrow, and we looked long at each other, and neither of us was afraid of the other.

And the Sparrow said within his heart, It is for Me that this building hath been erected, and this Statue lifted high, with this cozy place for a Shelter from the Storm. To this end did Christopher Columbus cross the Ocean, that he might have this Building named for him, and that I might have shelter.

Now when the bird spake thus in his heart, and I saw and understood the intent thereof, I did not chide the Sparrow, for I myself have had Just as Little Thoughts of the Providence of God and the Answer of my Prayers as the Sparrow. And while it was all Very Foolish, I am not so sure that it was as Foolish as it would have been to Stay out in the Storm till the Sparrow had learned for What Other Purpose Christopher Columbus crossed the Ocean, or for me to question too curiously What Larger Meaning there may be in the Providence of God.

Then said I, Oh my God, I am of more value than many Sparrows, but I do not know much more than they, and some men know less. The Sparrow hath found her an House, and the Swallow a Nest in the Protecting Shelter of Thine Altars, and they know not that those Altars have any Other Use. I do not know much more about Thy Providences than that Sparrow knoweth about Christopher Columbus, but I know that when the Blast of the Terrible ones is as a Storm Against the Wall, Thou dost keep him in Perfect Peace whose mind is stayed on Thee.

Crumbs and Bubbles

Now I was meditating on the things that seem to be Trivial and how when they are many, they become an Heap so that they Block the Amenities of Life.

And I listened and I heard the Patter of Little Feet, and I stopped my work, and the daughter of the daughter of Keturah ran into mine arms, and pulled my Beard, and kissed me upon both of my cheeks and once beside, and she said:

Grandpa, on this day I am Three Years Old, and behold there hath been given unto me a Doll, and a Cake with Three Candles thereupon.

And I said unto her, It was a glad day when God sent thy mother unto us, and another glad day three years ago when He did send thee; and behold the years have gone so fast that when I hold thee in mine arms, I know not if it be thee or thy mother.

And she said, Grandpa, Behold, it Snoweth. Take me out that I may behold the Snow.

So I took her out, wrapped in her Double Garments, and she rejoiced in the Snow. And she beheld how it came down in her face in what she called Little Bubbles, for they melted straightway, and how it fell upon my coat in what she called Little Crumbs.

For it is on this manner that she fitteth the words that she knoweth to her New Experiences, and oft do I marvel at the way in which she findeth a word for the thing she hath not known. And I considered her use of the words Bubbles and Crumbs of Snow. And we went within the house, and watched through the window, and we

saw the snow strike the window in Bubbles, and fall outside in Crumbs. And the Crumbs and the Bubbles were
both Very Little Things.

Now when the morning was come, behold the Snow
was piled at my door in a Great Drift. And I listened,
and behold there were no Trains, and I waited, and behold there were no Mails. And certain of my neighbors
had no Coal and could not get it.

And I considered, and said, Behold the Bubbles of
Snow and the Crumbs of Snow that fell in the face of the
Little Maiden, and on the Overcoat of her Grandfather.
How small were they one by one, and behold they Stop
the Trains.

And I considered that it is even so with many things in
life that are small in themselves, but when multiplied
they become Habits that men cannot break, or Griev-
ances that rend Friendships Asunder, even as Great Drifts
are made of Bubbles and Crumbs of Snow.

The Barber-Shop

I was grieved by the Follies and Sins of men. And it
seemed to me that all men were Wicked and all women
were Foolish. And there were certain days wherein there
came to me men and women whose deeds merited re-
proof. And I reproved them sharply; yea, I told them
every one his Sin.

And there followed a day which was the Sabbath. And
the thing had Got on my Nerve. And I went into the
Sanctuary, and I stood up in the sight of the Whole Con-

gregation, and I rebuked the people for their Backslidings and their Transgressions. And I feared not their faces; neither spared I them in my chastisement.

And certain of the congregation spake to me, saying, Thou dist Rub it in a Little Too Vigorously.

And I said, Nay. I speak as the prophets of God must speak. I will not prophesy smooth things. I will Cry Aloud and Show the people their Transgressions. Yea, the Word of God in my mouth shall not be as it were a Mouth of Meal, but as a two-edged Sword, dividing asunder the Joints and Marrow, and Discerning the Thoughts and Intents of the Heart.

Now on the morrow I said to Keturah, I go to the Barber-Shop.

And Keturah said, Go, my lord. But another time go thou on the day that precedeth the Sabbath; for thy hair and thy beard showed yesterday that they needed to be Trimmed.

So I went to the Barber-Shop. And I sat on a Great Throne, with a Bib about me, while the Barber did his Duty. And I beheld, and there hung before me a Leathern Case wherein were many Razors; and they were exceeding sharp. And upon the Shelf were many pairs of Shears. And beside these were certain pairs of Clippers.

And I said to myself, Here also is a man who needeth Sharp Instruments in his Business, even as I do.

And I Spake to the Barber, and I said, Behold, thou dost use in thy Business only the things that are Sharp.

And the Barber answered and said, Not on thy Life. Thou hast another Think Coming. The Razor and the Shears and the Clippers represent only a small part of my Equipment. I use Cold Cream that sootheth; and

Bay Rum that feeleth Mighty Good after a Shave; and Ointment that healeth wheresoever the Razor goeth over a place where the Skin hath any manner of Hurt. Yea, and I have Lotions and Talcum Powder, and Lots of Stuff to make a Fellow feel Good. Otherwise must I go out of Business. I could never run this Shop with Sharp Instruments Alone.

And I meditated much on what the Barber said to me.

And I said to my soul, If the Barber needeth Healing Lotions and Emollients in his Business, much more do I. I will not attempt hereafter to run my business with Sharp Instruments only.

And I knew that God had sent me to the Barber-Shop that I might learn this lesson. Yea, and also because I needed an Hair Cut.

And I told it to Keturah. And Keturah spake to me and said, Tell it to all men who Preach: for among them are Many Men who possess as Little Wisdom as doth my lord. Yea, and there may be a few who know even less.

On Duty Half Done

It was winter, and at Time of Snow. And some men Cleaned their Walks, and some did not.

And the Sun shone out, and some of the Snow Melted, and some did not. And then straightway did it Freeze again.

Now I have a neighbor who is always first to clean his walk. And I suspect that it is not because he feareth God or doth regard man, but that he may have wherewith to boast, and to vaunt himself against his neighbor.

And I came to his walk, and behold, the water had melted and run down upon it, and frozen so that it was like Glass. And I did very nearly break my neck in that place.

And on the next day I did meet him, and he spake ill concerning his neighbors. And he said, They have no Public Spirit, neither do they clean their walks; but my walk is clean.

And I said, Yea, it is clean, and it is the most Dangerous Walk in town. For they that left the snow, there may men walk safely; for that men's feet have trodden it roughly, and when it freezeth, then it is indeed a Hobbly Place, but men's feet slide not. But before a man setteth foot on thy walk, then should he buy more Accident Insurance, or a Gun.

And he said, What, dost thou reprove me for doing my duty, and for cleaning my walk?

And I said, For a good deed I reprove thee not. But know this, that the reward for the doing of one duty is the privilege of doing another; and he who cleaneth his walk so that it is slippery, should keep a Coal-hod of Sand wherewith to sprinkle the walk.

And he said, Dost thou make a virtue of the conduct of those who Lie in Their Beds while I shovel my walk?

And I said, I praise them not, neither do I think them virtuous. But there is no Vice like the half of a Virtue, nor any sin like a Duty half done.

The Catalogue of Flowers

Now there came to Keturah a Woman's Magazine. And it cometh once in Every Month. And the leaves of the Magazine bear Twelve Manner of Advertisements, one for every month.

And it came to pass that while the snow was deep upon the ground, behold she was reading advertisements of Flowers and Seeds. And there was one advertisement which said,

Send unto us a Dime and we will send to thee Six Packages of Seed, and a Wondrous Catalogue, and a Book that telleth thee All About the Garden. And Keturah sent the dime.

And when the Catalogue came, behold it was covered on the inside and on the outside with Flowers of Wondrous Beauty. And it told of many kinds of Flowers, yea, and of Vegetables that may be grown in the Back Yard and reduce the High Cost of Living. And there was a Coupon that said, Buy from us the value of a Dollar, and this Coupon shall be as it were Twenty-Five Cents of the Same.

And Keturah did that also.

But I said, Behold the ground is white with Snow, and deeply Frozen underneath it.

And she said, Yea, I know that the ground is white with Snow, and that there is deep Frost underneath it. But the Seed Catalogue is a Sign of Spring. Yea, and Spring beginneth in mine own heart when I begin to plan for the Garden.

And I considered the Hollyhocks that I had planted,

and which lay deep under the snow. And I wondered
how it fared with them, and whether there were Any
New Kinds.

And I said, Behold, there be many weary weeks before the Spring shall come, but I will send a Dollar with
that of Keturah, and I will plant Hollyhocks in mine
heart this day.

So will I not wait till Spring to possess mine Hollyhocks; for behold they are mine already: those in the
Seed Catalogue, and those that be under the Snow.

The Different Kinds of Seed

We made a Garden, I and Keturah, for so have our
forefathers done, even from the First of them, who was
Fired from his Job. And we made a place for Flowers,
and a place for Vegetables. And wherever there was
Room, there did I plant an Hollyhock.

And we made a Bed, with Straight Rows across it,
three hand-breadths apart, which is two parts of a Cubit.
And in the Rows I planted Seeds which I had bought
from the Vendor. And when the Envelope wherein the
seed came was Empty, then did I drive a Stake at the
end of the Row, and thereon I Stuck the Envelope.

And Keturah asked me, saying, Canst thou not remember that there be Three Rows of Radishes, and Two
of Lettuce, and one of Onions, and the Rest?

And I said, The Seeds are many, and they are very
Small. We must expect not Too Much of them. How can
each Seed know what it is to be? But now shall it know.

For if it cannot Read English, then may it look on the Envelope, and say, Behold I am to be like unto that Picture, and my name is Turnip.

And Keturah said, It is for thyself thou dost place the Envelope so, that thou mayest know the plants from the Label and conceal thine own Ignorance.

And I said, O Keturah, what is all the wisdom in the world save this, that by some tag or label placed here and there at the end of the Row, they that are wise conceal their Ignorance? For that Ignorance is very Vast, and it Shutteth Down about us on every side. There be men who know more about Seed than I do, so that they can tell a Radish Seed from a Lettuce Seed before they plant it. But who of them knoweth on the Law of Chances, that what seed Produced Radish last year shall not of the same kind of Seed produce this year Pumpkin Vines, each bearing in every Blossom a Pumpkin Pie?

So I entered into mine House, and I sat me down, for I was weary, and I meditated much that God needeth not the Labels to remind Him what each Seed shall produce. And I marveled at the Miracle of Life, that every seed doth bring forth after its kind, so that even the Grain of Mustard Seed hath in it a Great Tree, and every package of Seed doth contain the Memory of God, yea, and every tiniest seed the Veracity of God.

Now this human life is an Envelope, containing the Seed of a Nature which though it be mine own I understand but little. And I dimly Comprehend the Implications of Mine Own Soul when it seeketh to rise a little space above the Ground, and put forth Blossoms and Fruit. But I have felt within me Strong Impulses which Lift me Upward, and fashion Better Hopes in ways

Higher than mine own understanding. And it doth not yet appear what I shall be, but some things I know.

The Easter Bonnet

Keturah spake unto me, saying, The Spring hath come.

And I answered, I have heard the Lark, and seen the Robin, and I have some Hollyhock seed that I intend to plant.

And Keturah said, It is time for me to select a Spring Hat.

And I said, Thou hast a Spring Hat.

And she said, It is All Out of Style.

And I said, What should that matter, so long as it becometh thee?

And she said, It becometh me no more; it is not becoming in me to wear an Hat that is no longer in Style.

And I said, The Styles are Ridiculous.

And she said, Nay, they are fine; yet if they were Ridiculous, that were no good reason for not wearing them. Wearest thou not Stiff Bosomed Shirts and an Hat a Cubit in height, the same being the most ridiculous things that humanity ever wore?

And I said, Yea; but I wear my shirts until they are worn out; and my Hat requireth but one Ironing in a Year, and it lasteth alway.

And I said unto her, Last season's hats were ridiculous, and the year is well spent in that it showed to women how ridiculous they were. And next year's styles are ridiculous, as every man knoweth who seeth a new fashion plate before he seeth the apparel on the women folk he loveth to see Dolled Out. And the present year's fashions are ridiculous, but thou knowest it not.

And Keturah said, It is not knowing it that preventeth it from being ridiculous.

And she bought the Hat, and it is Ridiculous; but on her it is Mighty Becoming.

Hollyhocks I Did Not Plant

We lived three years in an hired house, both I and Keturah, while they builded the Synagogue. And it was a new house wherein never man had lived, and the Land about it was Untilled, and grown to Weeds. But we caused the Grass to grow, and Divers Flowers. Yea, and I brought thither Hollyhocks, even the Hollyhocks which the Municipal Mower cut down, and the Three Hollyhocks which it spared, and divers other Hollyhocks. And three sides of the Garden were walled about with them, so that when a Stranger came and asked, Where is the house of Safed the Sage? they would say unto him, Behold he dwelleth in the Place of the Hollyhocks.

Now the building of the Synagogue was finished, and the men of my congregation purchased an House that joined hard by the Synagogue, and I and Keturah we came there and abode. And it was Winter, so that we knew not what manner of flowers were planted there.

And when the Spring drew nigh, I spake often to Keturah, and said, The Hollyhocks that we planted where once the weeds were, behold they are ours no more.

And the warm winds blew from the South, and the
rains watered the earth, and there began to grow in the
Garden of the house hard by the Synagogue Little Young
Things that yet shall be flowers. Yea, and at the outer
side of the Garden, lo, there were Hollyhocks growing.
And there is a Window that openeth from the Room that
is mine own, and beside it I beheld that Young Hollyhocks were springing.

And I called unto Keturah, and she came, and I said,
Behold, the People who lived here before us were Good
People, who Feared God and loved Beautiful Things. Be-
hold the Hollyhocks whereon we have spent no labor.

And Keturah answered and said, Verily, this is the reward of right living, that one passeth on to those who
follow the fruits of the good which he doeth. For others
shall enjoy the Hollyhocks of our planting, and we shall
enjoy the Hollyhocks that were planted by those who
were here before us.

And I said, It is even so. And there are certain Good
People who have Hollyhock seed, and they will send of it
to me. And we will plant that also, and by the time we
are through, this place shall have Hollyhocks that grow as
Bulrushes grow in the land of Egypt.

For the Hollyhocks grew in Palestine, even in the land
where Jesus lived. And the seed thereof was brought into
the lands on the hither side of the Mediterranean by the
men who fought in the Crusades that they might win
back the Sepulchre of Jesus. And they called it the Holy
Hock.

Wherefore after I am dead and gathered to my fathers
shall men say when they come where I have lived, Behold these are the Hollyhocks that were planted by

Safed, whom some men called the Sage. And others will know nothing of Safed, but the Flowers will be there.

Hollyhocks I Transplanted

The Winter was long and cold, and the Spring came timidly. Divers were sick among the people whom I loved, and some of them died. And we took the Easter Lilies from the House of God and laid them upon the new graves of those who were dear to us. And I went often to the place appointed for the dead, and beside every grave did I speak words of comfort, and in every grave did I bury a part of mine own heart.

And I was weary and sad. And I said, Wherefore doth God take men away in the midst of their years? Why hath life so many sorrows?

And it was the first Spring in our new home. And I went to the house where formerly we did live, and I said unto the people that dwell there, Give me, I pray, of the Hollyhocks that I have planted here; for there be enough for me and for you.

And they said, Take what thou wilt; are they not thine own? And for what thou dost leave we are grateful.

So I digged among the Hollyhocks where they were thick, and took up those that were too Crowded. And I carried them carefully, and I brought them to the New Home that is hard by the House of God.

But the Hollyhocks wot not what I did, and they complained. And I listened to them, and they answered me, saying:

Behold thou didst plant us here, and we have grown and done well. Wherefore dost thou remove us? Do we not make this place Beautiful, so that we are instead of Weeds in this spot? And behold our Roots, how thou dost rend them, and lay them bare, and do them Violence. Why are thy ways unequal, and wherefore dost thou destroy the Hollyhocks of thine own planting?

And the Hollyhocks knew not that I had a place prepared for them, neither did they understand that they were to blossom more abundantly in my garden hard by the House of God.

The River Current

We sailed on the River, I and Keturah, yea, upon two Rivers, and even Three. For we entered into a Ship and sailed down the Mississippi, and up the Ohio, and then up the Tennessee. And we sailed for Eight Days, and we sailed for a Thousand Miles. And the waters in all these rivers were high, and the Current was swift. And we ascended the Tennessee slowly by reason of the Current. And I grew anxious, for I must needs return for the next Sabbath, and one Sabbath I had already been away.

And the Captain spake unto me saying, Fear not. We ascend slowly, but we shall go down the River like a Bat escaping out of Perdition.

And that was the way we came down.

And we neared a City the name whereof was Paducah, where three great rivers meet, even the Tennessee and the Cumberland and the Ohio. And I and Keturah we were to leave the boat there.

And the Captain came unto me, and he said, Behold, I was Mistaken. We shall hardly make thy Train.

And I said, Behold how fast we go, and Paducah is but Twenty Miles away.

And he said, Paducah is indeed but Twenty Miles away, but we are not Going Fast. We are burning Just as Much Coal, and the Wheels are Going around Just as Fast. But we are no longer in the waters of the Tennessee, but in the Backwaters of the Ohio. For the Ohio is rising More Rapidly than the Tennessee, wherefore the Mighty Current that bore us down hath ceased, and a Mightier Current all unseen doth Hold Us Back.

And I thought of the men who begin their Religious Life with a Strong Current of Love and Devotion moving with their Will and Mightily sweeping them forward toward their Desired Haven, but also of the Unseen Currents of Worldliness that Imperceptibly retard them, and even cause them to drift the Other Way.

And on the Sabbath I stood before my congregation, and I said, O men and women, think not because the Wheels still Go Around and thou art Puffing and Making Much Smoke that thou shalt surely go to Heaven. Behold there is an Undertow, and a Mighty Inflooding that may Hold thee Back, or even Drift thee whither thou wouldest not go.

These things I spake on the Sabbath, because in Spite of the Backwater, I and Keturah we Got There.

The First Robin

Now the Winter had been Long, and Very Cold, and
the Snow had been deep, and Spring was not yet come.
And I rose early in the morning, and I looked out of mine
Window, and Behold a Robin.

And I called unto Keturah, and said, Come quickly,
and see thou hasten thine arrival at the Window. For
here is a Friend of ours that is Come from a Far Country
to Visit us.

And Keturah came to the Window, and she also beheld the Robin.

Now the Robin looked at us, and hopped about upon
the Cold and Bare Ground, and looked for the Early
Worm, but the Bird was Earlier than the Worm. And Keturah went to her Kitchen to see what she might find that
the Robin would eat.

And I spake to the Robin, and said:

Behold, thou hast been where it was Warm and the
Sun did Shine. And thou couldest have stayed there. But
here thou art. And thou comest while it is yet Winter, for
the Prophecy of Spring is in thy Blood. Thy faith is the
substance of things hoped for and the evidence of things
not seen. Thou hast come many miles, yea hundreds of
miles, to a land that lies desolate, because thou hast within
thy soul the assurance that Spring is near. Oh, that
there were in human life some assurance that would send
men forth to their High Destiny with as compelling a
Conviction!

And I thought of the Eye, that it is formed in darkness,
but formed for the light; and the Ear that is wondrously

shaped in Silence, but made for the hearing of Music; and of the Human Soul that is born into a world where Sin is, yet born with an assurance of Righteousness.

And I blessed the Little Bird that had caused me to think of these things.

And I went forth among men that day, and they said, Salaam, Safed. Behold is it not a cold and long Winter?

And I said, Speak to me no more of Winter.

And they said, Wherefore should we not speak of Winter? Behold the Thermometer and the Empty Coal Bin.

But I held mine Head Proudly and I said:

Speak to me not of Winter. Behold, on this morning I did see the First Robin. For me henceforth it is Spring.

The Robin and the Cherries

There groweth a Cherry Tree hard by the house where I dwell, and in the Spring it was full of Blossoms, so that I wondered not at the people of Japan who rejoice with great joy in the Cherry Blossom time. And I was glad that George Washington did not pass that way in his boyhood. And after the blossoms came the Cherries, and they grew Wondrous Fast. And I said unto Keturah, We shall have no lack of Cherries.

And she said, Be not too sure. There be things that can happen to Cherries ere thou dost eat them.

Now ere the Cherries were ripe, I went to the window, and behold, a Robin in the Cherry Tree. And he sat so that he was nigh unto me, and he moved not away when I came nigh.

And I spake, saying, Behold, these Cherries are mine; moreover they are not yet ripe; and the Ground is full of Nice Juicy Worms; go thither and eat, and disturb not my Cherries.

And the Robin turned his head on one side, and pecked at a Cherry that was beginning to be Red, and then he turned his head the other way, and pecked at another.

And I said, Eat thou not of my Cherries, but eat Bugs; they are Excellent Substitutes; so shalt thou be nourished, yea, and please me also.

And the Robin spake unto me saying, Dost thou not remember the morning in Early Spring when first I came, and how thy heart did rejoice in me? And behold, I have builded my nest, and reared my young and fed them with worms which I took from thy Garden; and Now I am ready for Cherries.

And Keturah she came, and we stood there and talked unto the Bird, both of us, and the Robin was not affrighted, but listened to all we had to say, and still continually did he peck at the unripe Cherries.

And Keturah answered and said, There will be Cherries left for us, if we get out and pick them when they be first ripe; some of them will I can. Yea, and I will make for thee a Wondrous Cherry Pie, with all the Stones taken out. And as for the Robins, let them have their share. If I had to live on Worms for the Most Part of the Year, I should welcome the ripening of the Cherries.

And I looked at the red that was coming on the cheek of the Cherries and then at that on the breast of the Robin, and I said, Old fellow, Go to It. We will go Fifty-Fifty on those Cherries. There is no joy in life but doth

cost something, and the Robin is worth the Cherries he
doth eat.

The Height of the Sky

I have a little Granddaughter, and she is the daughter
of the daughter of Keturah. And on many days last summer she spake to me, saying, Grandpa, I want to Swing.
And whatsoever I was doing I did it no more, but I went
and Swung her.

Now on one of those days she looked up into the great
Pine Trees where the Swing was hung, and she asked me
Questions. And I showed her how the Trees divided into
Limbs, and the Limbs separated into smaller Branches,
and the Branches into Twigs, and the Twigs feathered
out into Delicate Pine Needles.

And all this she saw. And she saw that there was Blue
beyond the Tops of the Trees, which showeth in Marvel-
lous Beauty through the Tracery of the Pine Needles.
And she asked, Grandpa, what is that? And I told her
that the Blue above the tops of the Trees was the Sky.

And she looked long at the Sky, and it appeared Very
High as she saw it through the Treetops. And when she
saw How High it was, she considered, and she said:

But I can hardly reach it.

That was all she said of it, and she is not yet three
years old.

She could hardly reach it; even as the man of God in
olden time thought the Heaven and the knowledge of

God too wonderful for him and said, It is high; I cannot attain unto it.

And yet she did not say she could not entirely reach it. For the Sky beginneth not far above the treetops, but at the very ground; and the little damsel toucheth it with her fingertips all the day long. And they are such delicate little fingertips.

O my God, as the heaven is high above the earth, so are Thy Ways above our ways, and we can hardly reach Thee; yet do I thank Thee that Thou art not wholly out of reach. Thou art as near unto me as the Sky is nigh unto the little Maiden, and that is not quite out of reach.

Concerning Rest

There was a day when I was weary. For my days had been full of cares, and my nights had been broken. And I spake unto Keturah, saying,

I would fain lay me down upon my Couch and rest. Trouble me not for the Space of One Hour.

So I laid me down.

And I heard the Patter of Little Feet, and there were Little Hands pushing at my door. And there came unto me the daughter of the daughter of Keturah. And the little maiden is not yet three years old.

And she said, Grandpa, I want to lie down with you.

And I said, Come, and we will rest together. Close thine eyes Tightly and be Very Still. So shall we rest both of us.

And the way she rested was this. She crept under the

Blanket that covered me, so that her head and all the rest of her were Covered, and she said, Grandpa, you have losed your little girl.

Then did I seek my little girl whom I had losed, and I said, Where is my little girl? Where is my little girl? And I felt all over the Blanket, and I found her not.

Then did she cry, Here I am.

And she threw off the Blanket, and laughed.

And she hid from me the Second Time, and the Third Time, and Many Times beside. And every time I found her again, hiding under the Blanket.

And when this had wearied her, she Sat Astride me, so that One Foot was on the Right Side and one was on the Left, and she held me by the thumbs, and her little hands could not quite reach around my two thumbs. And she rocked back so that her head touched the couch between my knees, and she sat up with a Bump upon my Stomach. And she rode me to Banbury Cross and to many other places.

And she said, You are having a good time with me, aren't you, Grandpa?

And I told her that it was true.

Now at the end of One Hour, I came forth leading the little damsel by the hand, and Keturah said, Thou art rested. I behold that thy weariness is gone.

And it was even so. For the joy of playing with the little damsel had driven away my care, and I was rested.

Now I thought of this, and I remembered that my Lord had said unto me and not to me only but to all mankind, Come unto me, ye weary and heavy-laden, and I will give you rest. And I remembered He said that in resting I should bear a yoke and find it easy, and carry a

burden and find it light. And, behold, I knew what He
meant.

The Quick and the Dead

We went, I and Keturah, unto the Great Hall where
the Symphony Orchestra of an hundred men who have
skill play on Instruments of Musick.

And one said, This day there is to be a First Performance of a New Overture, and the Composer is a man of
this City. Come and meet him.

So I went and had speech with him.

And he was Nervously Awaiting his own number,
which was the Third, and the first two were long and
seemed to him longer.

And he opened his heart and told me many things.

And he said, I have lived all my life in hope of this
day. In my boyhood I loved Musick, and I worked hard
to earn money that I might study it. Then did I begin to
teach Piano and Violin and Voice. But now I teach only
Harmony. And all the years I have waited for the time
when a piece of mine own composing should be played
by the Symphony Orchestra, and I would lead it.

And he told me how long it took him to compose the
Overture, and how many times he wrote it; and how he
labored nights for Four Months to copy the scores for the
Orchestra Parts.

And it came to pass that his piece was rendered, and
he conducted it.

And it required Twelve Minutes. And for that he had worked Forty Years!

And at the end he was applauded. And they called him back thrice. And after all other men and women had ceased, still did I applaud him, and Keturah she also applauded, so that those about us joined in, and so we gave him one more come-back than the law required.

And Keturah said, I have never known thee to applaud so much.

And I said, This man is of mine own city and treadeth the same hard pavements that jar me. And he hath long taught reluctant pupils to play on the Psaltery and the Sackbut and the Dulcimer, all the while dreaming of this day. And his triumph lasteth just Twelve Minutes. Now the Lord do so to me and more also if I give him not all that is coming to him.

And Keturah said, But the rest of the program is of the Great Composers, even Liszt and Mozart and Mendelssohn. And thou didst applaud them but little.

And I said, If the Great Composers were living in this town and walked the floor nights with the baby, then would I applaud them more.

And I said, I also am in daily competition with the Mighty Dead. For men say, Why should we pay a Dollar for the Parables of Safed the Sage when we can buy Shakespeare and Bacon for an Half Dollar each? And Shakespeare and Bacon can now live on smaller royalties than I, and their wives need not new Easter Bonnets. Even so hath this man been all his life in competition with Liszt and Mendelssohn and Mozart. And he liveth in my town, and hath a name that is spelled like unto the way that it is pronounced.

And I said, I honor the Mighty Dead for their works' sake; but I will not blister my hands for them. I would rather applaud a Living American than a Dead Dutchman.

And the Intermission ended, and we heard a Symphonic Poem by Liszt. And him I applauded some and sufficient, but Liszt hath been dead some time, and there was another man who came back one time more because I and Keturah kept clapping.

The Next Time

There lived in the Town of my Boyhood a Damsel, whose name was Dinah. And I liked her, and knew not but that I could like her more if I were to Drop Everything Else and give her my Exclusive Attention.

And I went away and abode for certain months in another place. And Dinah came thither to visit, and I determined to Show her a Good Time, for she was from my Home Town. And Dinah was willing, but also was pursuing a policy of Watchful Waiting in certain other Directions.

And there came the Fourth Day of July, and the Sunday School Picnic. And some rode thither in Buggies, but the most part in Hayracks, or any old way. But I stood in with a man who had two Saddle Horses, and he was particular to whom he loaned them.

And when I came unto the house where she lodged, leading one horse and riding one, Dinah's countenance fell.

And she said, Safed, it is good of thee to take me to places, and I like it, but thou art only a boy from the Home Town, and I would fain ride in one of the loads, that I may meet others as well as thee.

And I went to a friend, who was driving his own two horses, that were hitched to an Hayrack. And beside him was his best girl, and her name was Ruth. And upon the Hayrack were young men and maidens.

And I said, Sam, wilt thou do me a Favor?

And he said, I will give thee anything, save Ruth only.

And I said, Take thou my two saddle horses for thee and Ruth, and let me drive thy team.

And he said, Let us hasten, Ruth, and climb down from here and mount the horses.

Now when Dinah saw that Ruth and Sam were glad, then was she more snippy than ever.

But that day was not wholly lost. For there rode on the Hayrack two maidens whom I had not met before.

And one of them was Keturah.

Now after fourteen years, Dinah wrote to Keturah, and said, I would visit thee.

And Keturah wrote and said, Come.

So she lodged with us four days. And she was still unmarried.

And on one night was a lecture. And Keturah cared not to go, but stayed with her Five Children, and I took Dinah to the lecture.

And as we were returning, Dinah spake to me, saying, Dost thou remember the Fourth Day of July, fourteen years ago?

And I told her that I had not forgotten.

And she said, When thou didst take me home that

night thou didst say to me, I am sorry that thou hast not enjoyed this day, and I hope it will fare better the Next Time I invite thee.

And I said, I remember.

And she said, Safed, this is the Next Time.

And I considered that some people who wait for the Next Time will have a long time to wait.

Hollyhocks and the Storm

There grow Hollyhocks at the home where we abode while they made ready for us the house hard by the Synagogue, for I planted them, and they will grow for many years. And now after two years there grow Hollyhocks at the house hard by the Synagogue. For I planted them, and when any friend of mine did send me seed, saying, Behold, here are Hollyhocks of a Choice Variety, then did I dig up another place for them and plant them there. And the time of blossoming drew nigh. And there came a mighty Rain, with a great Wind, and the Hollyhocks were Beaten Down so that they lay flat.

And I walked among them, I and Keturah, and she said, Behold how they begin to lift themselves again.

And I said, Yea, but I fear that they will not grow straight.

And Keturah put her hand under one of them, and lifted it gently, as she would have lifted a little child that had stumbled and fallen upon its face, and the Hollyhock stood up, albeit with soiled face and fingers, and

was erect. And she lifted another likewise. And she did
it gently.

And she said, Behold, they desire to rise, for God made
them upright. But when they get so far down, they must
be helped.

And Keturah said, My lord, it is even so with Folks.

And I said, Keturah, thou hast well said. It is hard
enough to stand erect when one hath never fallen. And
there are men and women who are down and think that
they are out, but are not, who need just the little lift
which thou art giving to these Hollyhocks.

And Keturah said, It is a sad thing for a flower that
hath the nature of a thing erect and beautiful, to be
beaten down so that it lieth in the mud, and hath no
comeliness or beauty; and it is only a little thing to lift it
up that it may grow. Yea, and if it need a stake that it
may have something to tie to, it is good use of timber.

Therefore did I and Keturah make a covenant with
each other and the Lord, that as we walk where the
storms of life have beaten, we will Lift Up every flower
of God that hath fallen across our path, and not trample
upon it nor despise it, but seek to make it fit to bloom in
the Garden of God.

The Signal Tower

The train whereon I rode drew nigh unto a City, and it
Slowed Up in the outermost parts thereof till the man in
the Signal Tower bade it go on. For he lived in a place
High and Lifted up, with Levers on this side of him and

on that, and with Electric Signals and many Strange Devices. And when he dropped the Semaphore, then did we go forward, not on a straight track, but we curved to the Right, and again to the Left, and we Smelled Out, as it were, the way that he desired us to go among the tracks till we came at length into a Great Terminal where a place had been prepared for us. And all the way, though we no longer saw him, his hand did guide the way whither we went, so that we smashed into no other train, though many were coming and going, but we came safely to our Desired Destination.

Now as we pulled slowly past the Signal Tower, I took note, and behold, it was in a Desolate Spot, where the Signal Man had Very Little Companionship. But he had climbed down in the hours when no trains were going, and had planted seeds about the Signal Tower. And there were Larkspurs to match the sky, and Poppies that grew red. And beside all these were Hollyhocks, yea and many of them.

There were Hollyhocks of Brown, like unto the eyes of Keturah, and Hollyhocks of pink, like her cheeks when first God gave her to me, and others white as the snow, and others red as the rose. And they grew ever upward as if they would mount to the Signal Tower and smile in at its windows at the man who planted them.

And as we went on our way, I thought of the man in the Signal Tower, and I said to him in my heart:

Thou art my brother. I also have a tower like unto thine, which appertaineth unto my Church, and there do I spend long hours in a place of mine own, apart from men and lifted up, that I may catch if so it may be the messages which I shall transmit into signals for them, to

keep them on the right track, and I also grow Hollyhocks.

So I climb again to my Signal Tower, and I seek if I
may give unto men the right Signals that they go aright
on life's course to their safe place in its Terminal; but also
will I brighten the earth beneath with Hollyhocks.

The Circus Procession

Now the daughter of Keturah spake unto me, saying,
Father, behold, there cometh a Circus to town. Wilt thou
borrow my Little Daughter and take her thereto?

And I said, Among the many uses of little children, one
is this, that by reason of them it becometh the duty of
Grandfathers to attend the Circus.

And we went early, but we did not avoid the Rush.

Now, we went behind the tents to where they made
ready for the Great Parade. And there were Famous Char-
acters of History in their Chariots, and there was a Cal-
liope that played Keep the Home Fires Burning on
Steam Whistles, and there were Very Funny Clowns, but
not so Funny as Clowns were when I was a Lad. And
there were Wild Beasts, as many as went into the Ark.

And there were Nine Elephants.

Now, the Elephants were Timid, and they liked not to
go in Procession. Therefore did their Trainer take an Old
Elephant, and set him in the front with a Mahout on his
head; and he commanded another Elephant to come forward and take with his Trunk the Tail of the First Elephant. Then did he bring forward the Third Elephant,

and command him to take hold of the Tail of the Second
Elephant. Likewise did he with all.

And the Elephants were no longer Timid, but walked
every one of them in the big, broad footsteps of the one
before him, and held every Elephant to another's tail.

Now when the daughter of the daughter of Keturah
saw this, she was Greatly Amused; and she Laughed,
and I laughed with her. For the Elephants were so large
and the tails which they clung to were so small.

And I said, My little maiden, what thou seest is a
Parable, and even such is Life. Men and Women who are
Old Enough and Big Enough and ought to Know Better,
stand trembling even like those Great Beasts till they
have some Slender Thing to Cling to whereby they may
follow in the Procession, not knowing whither they go.

But the little maiden listened not to my Moral. Wherefore did we go and buy Peanuts to feed the Elephants
when they returned, and some Pink Lemonade and a
Red Balloon for ourselves.

And it was a Good Show, but not such as they had
when I was a Lad.

The Bumble Bee

We came, I and Keturah, to the place where we are
wont to spend our Summers. And we walked under the
great Pine Trees, and I went with uncovered head, for I
reverence them. And we came nigh unto the nest of a
Bumble Bee, and I knew it not. And a Bumble Bee flew
at me Furiously, and he assailed my Head, and he thrust
out his Sting.

And Keturah saw him, and she cried out, Alas, my husband, for he hath stung thee on the Forehead.

And I answered and said, I am very grateful to that Bumble Bee.

And she said, Hasten and put something on it, ere it swell.

And I said, My head is not Swelled, neither shall that Bumble Bee swell it. He stung me not, and I am very thankful to him.

And she said, If he stung thee not, I am glad. But I know not why I should be thankful. For it was in his heart to sting.

And I said, My hair groweth thin, and my friends say, Safed groweth toward Baldness. But this Bee got Tangled in my Hair. He that hath hair enough to entangle a Bumble Bee is not Bald.

And I considered how many are the annoyances of life, and even of its threatened dangers, that afford us ground for joy, if we only know how to interpret them.

The Potato Bug

There came unto me a man, who sat him down before I asked him to do so. And he inquired of me, saying, Dost thou believe in Prayer?

Now, I am a man of Prayer, neither hath there been a day since my childhood when I have not prayed unto my God. But I answered him not, for I knew that he had not come to learn what I believed about Prayer, but to tell me what he believed, and that he would Never Notice whether I answered him or no.

And he took up his parable and said, I was on the
train, on my way to a Very Important Business Engage-
ment; and if I made it, I should make Good Money, and
give unto the Lord a tenth thereof. And my train was
late. And I approached a Junction. And if the other train
had gone, I had Missed my Appointment. So I took the
matter to God in prayer, and behold, the other train was
later than mine own. So did I meet the appointment, and
I sold the Goods, and the Treasury of the Lord shall pros-
per.

And he thought not of the many people on the Connecting Train who suffered by the delay which his
Prayer had Seemed to Produce.

And I said unto him, There is a place where I go in
Summer, where there are Trees and a Lake and Streams.
And there grew a Great Tree by the side of a stream, and
the waters washed under the roots upon the one side
thereof, so that the Tree grew out over the Stream. And
it was a Beautiful Tree, and it grew for an Hundred Years.
And the Cattle rested under the shade thereof, and the
Birds of Heaven did build their Nests in the branches
thereof.

Now, upon the one side of the Stream was there a
Potato Patch, and within the Patch there grew a Potato
Vine, and upon the Potato Vine there Crawled a Potato
Bug. And when the Potato Bug had filled his Belly with
the leaves of the Potato Vine, he looked across the
Stream, and behold there was another Potato Patch, fairer
than the one wherein he abode. And he said, I will go
forth, even unto that other Potato Patch, and there shall
my soul Delight itself in Fatness. So he came to the
Stream, and he could not get across. And he tarried there

that night. And in the night there arose a Great Wind, and it smote the Tree, so that it fell, and its Mighty Trunk lay across the stream. And when the morning was come, the Potato Bug climbed upon a root of the Tree, and he crossed over, and came unto the other side, and he went to the other Potato Patch. And he said, Now do I behold the Goodness of God who hath made a Bridge for me, and brought me safe over the Stream; for this is an answer to my Prayer. And while the Potato Bug gave thanks to God, the Cattle mourned for the Shade which had sheltered them, and the Birds were Sorrowing over their Broken Eggs, and over their Little Birds that were Crushed, and over their Homes that were Desolate. But the Potato Bug knew it not, nor regarded it, but thanked his God for the answer of the Prayer of the Potato Bug.

Now the man who had come to tell me that he believed in Prayer heard this parable, and he was wroth. And he said, Dost thou compare me to a Potato Bug?

And I said unto him, I speak the truth in parables; for the good God hath made the outer world and the things therein that they may be as a Mirror to the Souls of men. I do not compare thee to a Potato Bug, but if thou seest any Points of Similarity, that is thine own affair.

And he departed.

The Four-Cent Birthday

The daughter of the daughter of Keturah is three years of age, and she goeth upon the Sabbath Day unto the

Sunday School. And on every Sabbath she taketh with her a Nickel, the value whereof is Five Cents.

And it came to pass upon a Sabbath morning that she spake to her mother, and she said, Give me not Five Cents, I pray thee, but rather give me Four.

And her mother did even as she desired.

And upon that day she came home from the Sunday School in Great Glee.

And on the next Sabbath her mother gave unto her a Nickel, but she said, Nay, for I desire Four Cents.

And her mother said unto her, Wherefore dost thou desire Four Cents?

And she said, In order that I may have a Birthday.

And her mother said, Thou art but Three, and thy Birthday is not long past. It will be many months before thou shalt have a Birthday.

But she said, Nay, I had one last Sunday, and I must have another today.

Then said her mother, Didst thou indeed tell the Teacher that last Sabbath was thy Birthday?

And she answered, Verily I told her so, and I had the Four Cents. For whatsoever little girl doth bring Four Cents, she shall have a Birthday.

And her mother said, Nay, my daughter, it is not thus. Birthdays come not so often, and when they come thou must take them, even though the time shall come when thou wouldest give Four Cents not to have them. Take thy Five Cents.

And the Little Damsel answered, and said, If I take Five Cents the Teacher doth accept it and say nothing. But if I take Four Cents, then may I drop them one by one while all the children count thus, One, Two, Three,

Four. Yea, and they join hand to hand and march around
me, and sing a little Song concerning me. But if I take
Five Cents they do none of those things. Wherefore will
I take Five Cents no more, but rather will I take Four
Cents and have a Birthday every Sabbath.

Now when I heard these things I smiled. For verily I
have seen many people older than the daughter of the
daughter of Keturah who work the same Stunt success-
fully. Yea, they go through life making their Meager
Contribution but causing the Pennies to be counted so
conspicuously that the Great Overgrown Kindergarten
which is called The World doth join hand to hand and
sing a song around them.

But no man hath attained to Real Nobility of Soul till
he hath learned to drop in his Nickel and go on about his
business unpraised rather than enjoy the Cheap Fame
of the Four-Cent Birthday.

Out and In

There came to see me a man from another city, and it
is a Goodly City. And it lieth toward the Rising of the
Sun. And I met him on the Threshold of my House. And
he said,

Doth Safed the Sage live here?

And I told him that it would do him no good to seek
farther.

And he said, I have read of thee, and I had business
out here, and I have come to see thee.

And I asked him, Where didst thou say thou hadst
business?

And he said, I have business in thy city.

And I said, I understood thee to say that thou didst have Business Out Here.

And he said, I believe I did say so. In the city where I live, if a man come toward this point of the Compass, he speaketh of it as Out.

And I said, That form of speech showeth an Unfortunate Mental Attitude.

And he said, It is only a Form of Speech.

And I said, Nay, it is a Trait of Mind. The Chinese do teach in their Schools a science called Geography, wherein China is shown as the Middle Kingdom, with all other nations Outside, so that whithersoever a native of China goeth, he goeth Out, and whosoever cometh to China, he cometh In. It is more than a Form of Speech; it is a Mental Habit, and a Bad One.

And I said, God's sun knoweth no Out or In anywhere in the Temperate Zone, for every land hath its Morning and Noon and Night. He who thinketh of himself as going Out when he goeth to another city shutteth his Soul against some possibility of Instruction.

And he said, I do not think it is so bad as that. It is just our habit of speech. Nevertheless, I do verily believe that thou art right, and that no man in going from the East to the West or from the West to the East should speak of it as Going Out, lest he give offense.

And I said, That is not the Principal Reason; he should not speak thus because it conduces a Mental Limitation. East and West are both alike to the Sun, and each spot hath its own High Noon midway between Sunrise and Sunset.

And I said, This is In.

And he said, I verily believe that thou art right.

And I opened my door wide, and I said, Come In.

And he came In, and we had Sweet Fellowship together.

For he was a Fine Man, and all he needed to know was that he had not come Out but In.

Golf Ball and Earthquake

There came one to me and said, O Safed, I am told that thou art a wise man and also a righteous man.

And I answered, The two are not wholly incompatible; if men say such things concerning me I must be the more unmindful of my folly and my unworthiness.

And he said, Dost thou believe in the power of prayer?

Forasmuch as he knew very well what I believed, I answered him as I answer men when I desire that they shall make the Next Move. And I said unto him, Whether thou hast come to be enlightened, or hast come to enlighten me, say on, for the sunlight is scarce.

And he said, I believe that God answereth every true prayer. Dost thou so believe?

And I answered, Yea; and sometimes He answereth Yea, and sometimes He answereth Nay.

And he said, There is no Nay with the Almighty when the prayer of faith is answered.

And I said, It is well that all men pray, and that they pray the prayer of faith. But the prayer of faith is still the prayer of human understanding; and although the faith be perfect, the wisdom may be scant. Wherefore, if God

must needs say Yea to every fool prayer, then would I
desire to move into Some Other Universe. For I do verily
believe that God doth not loan His Rubber Stamp to
every strong-faithed and weak-minded Christian.

And he said, Cannot God turn our folly into wisdom?

And I answered, God can do everything that denieth
not His own nature and that involveth no contradiction of
terms. But some things that God can do, God is too good
and too wise to do, even though all the foolish Christians
on earth do tease Him.

And I said, There was a great game of Golf, wherein
the two players came to the Eighteenth Hole with an
even score. And one struck with his Putter and knocked
the ball so that it stopped just at the edge of the Hole.
And the other took his Putter and lifted it that he might
Putt, when there came a very small Earthquake, and the
ball of the other player Rolled In. And the question was
Much Discussed whether he did thereby win the game.
And they who were wise in matters of Golf decided that
a player may not Shake the Earth in order to Jar his Ball
into the Hole. And they gave the Game unto the other
man.

And I said, So is it with God. He hath placed this
Earth on the Tee, and hath knocked it over a Rocky
Course of Eighteen Holes with an hundred years to each
and then some. And He will yet land it in the Last Hole
by a Clean and Fair Stroke, and not by Violating the
Laws which He Himself hath made.

The Lost Affections

Now there came unto me a Middle-Aged Woman; and she said, Hast thou a Philosopher's Stone wherein thou dost look, and tell Unhappy People what to do?

And I told her that I had.

And she seated herself before me, and I looked at the Rings on her left hand and I looked also into the Philosopher's Stone, and I said, Thou art Married.

And she answered and said, I am.

And I looked again, and I said, Thou art unhappy.

And she said, O Safed, thou art indeed a man of Great Discernment.

And I said, Thy husband, who once was most fond, now Tendeth to his Business, and seemeth to thee to be Inconsiderate.

And she gently Sobbed her Assent.

And she said, O Safed, I simply must tell some one! And I have come to thee, for thou art Wise and Sympathetic. My husband once loved me Devotedly; it was Just Too Sweet for Anything, the Way he Loved me. But now I am Losing his Affections.

And she said, O Safed, dost thou not know some Philter, which I may cunningly concoct and give to him, that he may Partake Thereof and Love me Like he Used to?

And I answered, I know a Potent Love Potion, and I can impart it to thee.

And she said, O Safed, deceive me not, neither keep me Waiting!

And I said, This is the Potion. Go thou to the Market, and there get thee a Beefsteak An Inch Thick, and be

sure that it is Tender. Rub it gently with an Onion, and
put it in the Broiler, and be sure that the Broiler is Hot.
Place it over an Hot Fire and Cook it upon the one
side: then turn thou it and Cook it upon the Other Side.
And be sure thou cook it Quickly that thou cook the
Juice into it and not out.

And she said, I will tell the Maid to do it so.

And I said, Nay, but do it with thine own hands.

And she said, Is that all?

And I said, Sprinkle it lightly with salt, and yet more
lightly with Pepper; and place on the top thereof a Good
Big Lump of Butter. And take thou a Great Potato, and
Bake it with the Cover on; and when it is baked, open it
upon the Top Side, and put therein a Lump of Butter,
and some Salt, and sprinkle the edges with Red Paprika.
And bake the Potato first that thy Steak cool not while it
baketh. And have on thy Good Dress, which thou mayest
cover with a Big Gingham Apron; and when thou seest
thy husband coming, slip off thine Apron, and come to
the table in thy Best Bib and Tucker, and Smile at him
while he eateth thy Magic Potion.

And she said, Will that assuredly give me back my husband's affections?

And I said, It is warranted never to fail.

And she said, But what about the High Cost of Living?

And I said, The High Cost of Living is justified by
the High Cost of Loving. Beefsteak and Baked Potatoes,
though they come high, are cheaper than Divorce and
Alimony. Yea, and they yield their Peaceable Fruits.

And she went and concocted the Magic Potion even as
I told her. And she administered it to her husband Many
Times.

And they lived together Happily Ever After.

Sympathy and Helpfulness

There came to our City a Great Plague, even the Influenza.

And people that I knew not sent for me, saying, There lieth one dead in our house. Come, and speak to us a Word of Comfort, and pray to God on our behalf.

And I went to a House where the man had died. And his wife wept bitterly. And the women, her neighbors, gathered about her and sought to comfort her. Now the house was in Disorder; for the woman had never been a good housekeeper, though she loved her husband, and Lamented him sore.

And she cried, saying, Alas, my husband! He was all that I had! And we were very happy together, and now I am Desolate and Alone!

And the other women crowded about her, and essayed to comfort her. And they said, Weep not so sorrowfully, for verily thou shalt grieve thyself unto Sickness.

And she said, I care not that I should be sick; yea, I desire that I may be sick and die, and lie down beside him whom I loved.

And they said, Speak not thus Despairingly, nor be overcome of Grief.

But none of them Made up the Beds, nor Washed the Dishes, nor Dusted the Parlor Table.

And I spake of it to Keturah.

And I said, Sympathy is one of the most blessed things in life; yet do I prefer a sympathy that is helpful.

And Keturah said, Those neighbor women gave to her what she most needed. The unmade beds and the unwashed dishes did offend thine eye, but not hers nor theirs. The soul hath its deeper needs than dishwashing.

And I answered, Verily thou hast spoken truly. Nevertheless, I like better the sympathy that knoweth how to help.

The Needs of Great Men

We went, both I and Keturah, unto another city; and there we attended a Convention. And the people of that City were given to hospitality, and they received us into their homes, hoping to entertain Angels unawares.

And the Hostess of the Home where I and Keturah lodged spake privately unto Keturah, and she said,

Behold, all that we have is thine, and thy husband's. And I stand much in fear lest we be not able to do for thy husband what should be done unto him. For we have heard that he is a man of Distinction.

Now no one knoweth how little Distinction I have so well as Keturah, nor how little I deserve that little; but Keturah will never divulge that unto another, though she remind me of it in private.

And this woman spake unto Keturah, and told her what things she had heard concerning the husband of Keturah. And she said, I fear lest I be not able to do for him what should be done for so Distinguished a man.

And Keturah spake unto her comfortingly. And Keturah said, A Distinguished man needeth a bed no longer nor wider than any other man, nor a bath tub any more commodious. As among women the Colonel's lady and Judy O'Grady have all the essentials of their nature in common, so it is with men. Give unto a man three things, and he will do very well. Give him a comfortable place to sleep, and feed him well three times in the day, and make not too much fuss over him, and he will think that he is having a good time.

And our hostess said, Why, that is exactly what I do for mine own husband.

And she did even as Keturah said. And we were very happy in that place.

On Growing Old

Keturah spake unto me, and inquired of me, saying, Wilt thou love me when I am old?

And I answered, I will not.

And Keturah said, Verily thou didst promise.

And I said, I promised nothing of the kind, neither will I perform it. I promised to love the woman whom I married, and she was a young woman, and thou art that woman. Wherefore then should I love a woman who is old?

And she said, But, alas, my husband, I am not young as when I married thee.

And I said, If the years have done anything to thee, they have done the same to me, and I see thee no different, only more dear and more fair. Yea, and when many women are gathered in any place, then do I look around till I find the fairest of them all, and that is thee.

For I have always loved fair women and no others, and I
am too old to want any other kind. Therefore do I love
thee more than all else.

And Keturah said, Thou speakest like the foolish lover
whom thou hast ever been; and inasmuch as I have thee
fooled, it were greater folly to seek to make thee wise.
God grant thou be ever as foolish as thou art now.

And I said, O Keturah, I am not unmindful of what the
years have wrought in both of us. Thou art the mother of
men tall and strong, and of a daughter who is older than
thou wert when first God gave thee to me. Thou didst
not wear glasses when first I knew thee, neither was
there a gray hair in thy brown and waving hair, and thy
dark eyes looked at me from under a smooth brow. I do
verily see in thee some marks of physical change, and I
welcome them not either in me or in thee, for mine is an
heart of youth, and I delight not in anything that di-
minisheth strength. Yea, I dread the time when I shall
have to be careful what I eat, and when I shall be ad-
monished to take life less strenuously, for that I am no
longer young. And I rejoice now as a strong man to run
a race, neither do I know sickness nor weariness nor
pain. But I suspect that the years have left some mark
upon us both, only I see it not in either of us. And thou
art more fair to me than ever, yea, and ten thousand
times more dear.

And I said, Age dependeth not on how long a man
hath been born, for some men were old from their birth.
The angel that rolled the stone away from the tomb of
the dear Lord Christ had been in heaven ten thousand
years, but the women saw him, and had he been old they
would have noticed it; but he was a young man.

And I said, Keturah, if thou art any older than when I married thee, I do not suspect it.

And Keturah said, Just for that I will make thee a Cherry Pie; and my Cherry Pies are as good as when we first were married.

And I said, Yea, and I thank God that my appetite for them is as good as it was then.

And I might just mention that it was Some Pie.